CHRISTMAS MEDLEYS
FOR PIANO SOLO

Arranged by

JASON LYLE BLACK
"The Backwards Piano Man"®

ISBN 978-1-70510-525-2

Visit Hal Leonard Online at
www.halleonard.com

Contact us:
Hal Leonard
7777 West Bluemound Road
Milwaukee, WI 53213
Email: info@halleonard.com

In Europe, contact:
Hal Leonard Europe Limited
42 Wigmore Street
Marylebone, London, W1U 2RN
Email: info@halleonardeurope.com

In Australia, contact:
Hal Leonard Australia Pty. Ltd.
4 Lentara Court
Cheltenham, Victoria, 3192 Australia
Email: info@halleonard.com.au

ARRANGER NOTES

The Christmas holidays are one of my favorite times of the year! In approaching this book, as with my previous medleys, I wanted to capture the spirit of the originals, but with my own unique "spin."

I'm particularly fond of the Bossa Nova-flavored "Feliz Navidad"; the quick swing of "Deck the Halls" and "(Everybody's Waitin' For) The Man with the Bag"; the quiet tenderness of "Mistletoe"; and the fun Ragtime in "Rockin' Around the Christmas Tree."

My favorite in this book, though, is "Santa Claus Is Coming to Town." I get chills with the climactic ending, which draws on my experience as a jazz trumpet player. Can you just picture a 17-piece jazz ensemble playing it onstage? I can!

To provide arrangements for a variety of skill levels, I've intentionally varied the difficulty throughout the book. You'll also find two advanced "alternate endings" for extra adventure! If you enjoy this book, check out my *Disney Medleys for Piano Solo* as well (HL00242588).

Finally, I hope you'll come see me on tour! You can see tour dates on my website and social media channels. Also, be sure to check out my recordings of my Hal Leonard arrangements on YouTube.

Merry Christmas!

Jason Lyle Black

Find my videos here:
www.jasonlyleblack.com
youtube.com/jasonlyleblack
facebook.com/jasonlyleblack
Instagram: @jasonlyleblack

THE CHRISTMAS SONG/IT'S BEGINNING TO LOOK LIKE CHRISTMAS/THE MOST WONDERFUL TIME OF THE YEAR

Arranged by
JASON LYLE BLACK

Slowly and freely, with rubato (♩ = 72)

THE CHRISTMAS SONG
Music and Lyric by MEL TORMÉ and ROBERT WELLS

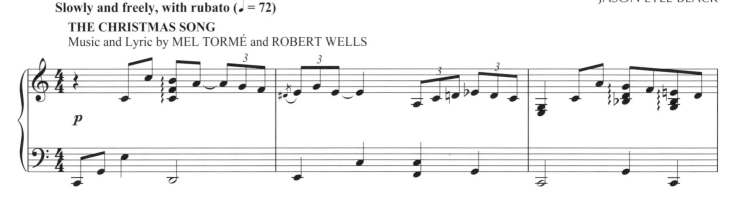

A little faster (♩ = 84)

THE CHRISTMAS SONG (Chestnuts Roasting on an Open Fire)

Quickly (♩ = c.120)
IT'S BEGINNING TO LOOK LIKE CHRISTMAS
By MEREDITH WILLSON

6

Briskly (♩. = c.60-64)

THE MOST WONDERFUL TIME OF THE YEAR
Words and Music by EDDIE POLA and GEORGE WYLE

emphasize the melody

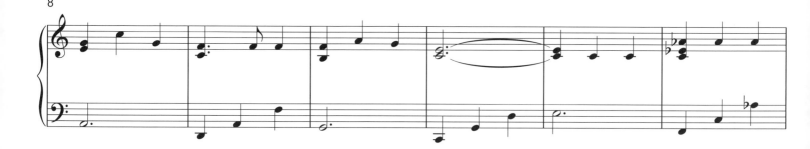

9

Slow and rubato, flexible rhythm (♩ = 60-64)
THE CHRISTMAS SONG

DECK THE HALLS/BABY, IT'S COLD OUTSIDE/WINTER WONDERLAND

Arranged by
JASON LYLE BLACK

DECK THE HALLS
Traditional Welsh Carol

Slowly, let it sway (♩ = 56)

BABY, IT'S COLD OUTSIDE
By FRANK LOESSER

Bring out the melody

WINTER WONDERLAND
Words by DICK SMITH
Music by FELIX BERNARD

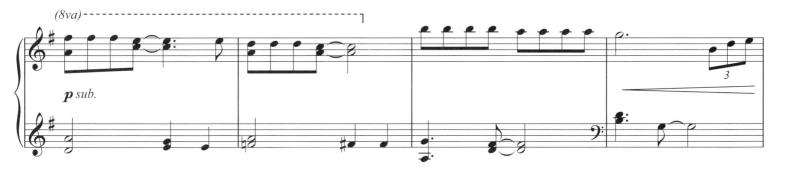

HAVE YOURSELF A MERRY LITTLE CHRISTMAS/I'LL BE HOME FOR CHRISTMAS

Arranged by
JASON LYLE BLACK

Slowly and expressively (♩ = c.76)*
I'LL BE HOME FOR CHRISTMAS
Words and Music by KIM GANNON and WALTER KENT

More motion (♩ = c.80)
HAVE YOURSELF A MERRY LITTLE CHRISTMAS
Words and Music by HUGH MARTIN and RALPH BLANE

This entire piece is rubato. Fluctuations in tempo and expression are key here.

More motion (♩ = c.90-96)
I'LL BE HOME FOR CHRISTMAS

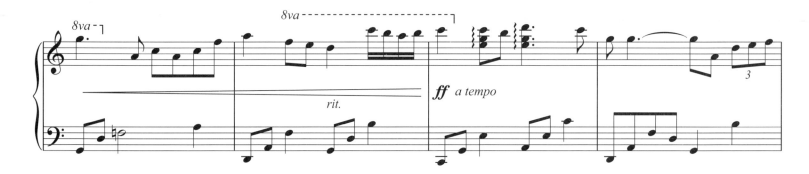

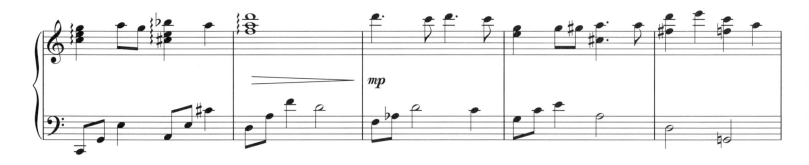

MISTLETOE/CHRISTMAS (BABY PLEASE COME HOME)

Arranged by
JASON LYLE BLACK

Cheerfully, slight Swing (♩ = c.72)

MISTLETOE
Words and Music by JUSTIN BIEBER, NASRI ATWEH and ADAM MESSINGER

Pedal ad lib.

*Keep pedal down throughout (change every two bars)

Slower, still Swing (♩ = c.64) (♫ = ♪♪³)
CHRISTMAS (BABY PLEASE COME HOME)
Words and Music by PHIL SPECTOR, ELLIE GREENWICH and JEFF BARRY

More quickly (♩ = c.68-72) (♫ = ♩♪³)

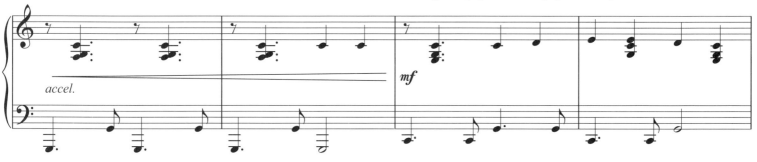

MISTLETOE

Straight 8ths

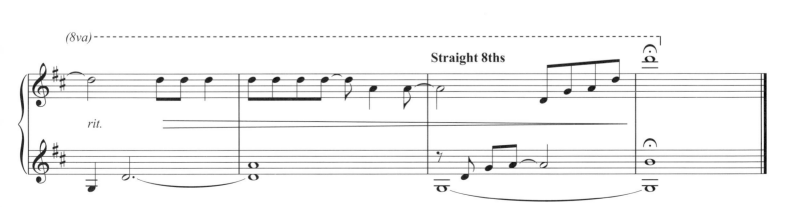

A HOLLY JOLLY CHRISTMAS/JINGLE BELL ROCK/ALL I WANT FOR CHRISTMAS IS YOU

Arranged by
JASON LYLE BLACK

Moderate Swing (♩ = c.144)

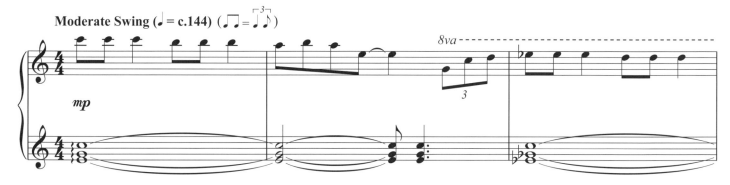

A HOLLY JOLLY CHRISTMAS
Music and Lyrics by JOHNNY MARKS

Keep steady (♩ = c.144)
JINGLE BELL ROCK
Words and Music by JOE BEAL and JIM BOOTHE

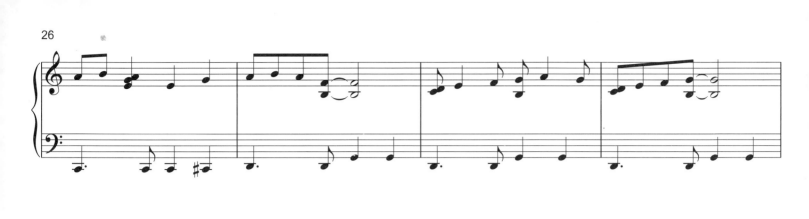

cresc. poco a poco

Continue Swing (♩ = c.148-152)

f

ALL I WANT FOR CHRISTMAS IS YOU
Words and Music by MARIAH CAREY and WALTER AFANASIEFF

mf

mp

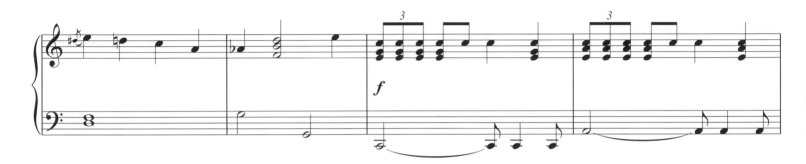

LET IT SNOW!/ROCKIN' AROUND THE CHRISTMAS TREE/SANTA CLAUS IS COMIN' TO TOWN

Arranged by
JASON LYLE BLACK

Very slowly, free rhythm (♩ = 90)

Quick Swing (♩ = 140-148)

cresc. poco a poco

LET IT SNOW! LET IT SNOW! LET IT SNOW!
Words by SAMMY CAHN
Music by JULE STYNE

cresc. poco a poco

Lightly, same tempo
ROCKIN' AROUND THE CHRISTMAS TREE
Music and Lyrics by JOHNNY MARKS

mf

p sub.

mf

33

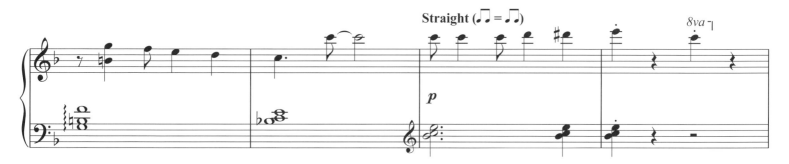

Straight (♪♪ = ♪♪)

Quick and fun (♩ = 172-180)

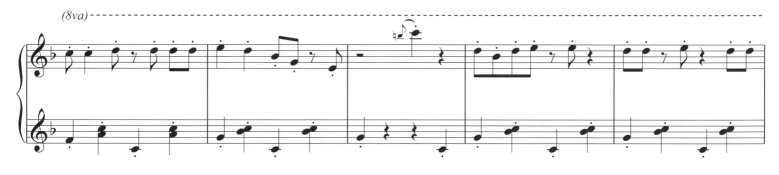

Still straight 8ths

Much slower (♩ = c.116)

mp

Swing! (♫ = ♩♪)

fp   *cresc. poco a poco*
       accel. poco a poco

Quick! (♩ = c.86)

SANTA CLAUS IS COMIN' TO TOWN
Words by HAVEN GILLESPIE
Music by J. FRED COOTS

f

cresc. poco a poco

*Optional: cut to
Alternate Ending*

Original Ending

ff

**Alternate Ending
(for advanced players)**

ff

cresc. poco a poco

R.H. tip: Use thumb for both bottom notes.

MARY, DID YOU KNOW?/ THE LITTLE DRUMMER BOY/ DO YOU HEAR WHAT I HEAR

Arranged by
JASON LYLE BLACK

Meditatively (♩ = c.96-100)

MARY, DID YOU KNOW?
Words and Music by MARK LOWRY and BUDDY GREENE

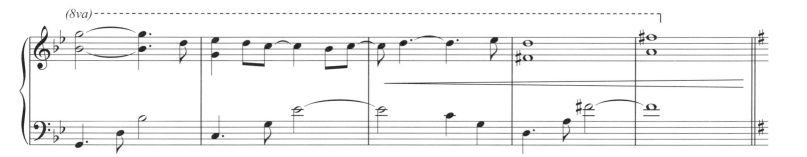

THE LITTLE DRUMMER BOY
Words and Music by HARRY SIMEONE, HENRY ONORATI and KATHERINE DAVIS

Slightly faster ($\quarternote$ = c.112)

A bit slower (♩ = c.104)
DO YOU HEAR WHAT I HEAR
Words and Music by NOEL REGNEY and GLORIA SHAYNE

PLEASE COME HOME FOR CHRISTMAS/(EVERYBODY'S WAITIN' FOR) THE MAN WITH THE BAG

Arranged by
JASON LYLE BLACK

Slow and easy (♩. = 60-64)
PLEASE COME HOME FOR CHRISTMAS
Words and Music by CHARLES BROWN and GENE REDD

Swing! With animation (♩ = c.88) (♫ = ♪♪)

(Everybody's Waitin' For) THE MAN WITH THE BAG
Words and Music by HAROLD STANLEY, IRVING TAYLOR and DUDLEY BROOKS

49

RUDOLPH THE RED-NOSED REINDEER/WE WISH YOU A MERRY CHRISTMAS/FELIZ NAVIDAD

Arranged by
JASON LYLE BLACK

Freely (♩. = 72)
RUDOLPH THE RED-NOSED REINDEER
Music and Lyrics by JOHNNY MARKS

Swing! (♩ = 80-88)

Now in rhythm

Moderately (♩ = c.144) (♫ = ♫)
WE WISH YOU A MERRY CHRISTMAS
Traditional English Folksong

Straight 8ths

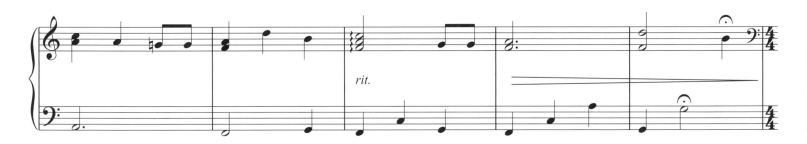

Slightly faster (if desired)

p sub.

pp

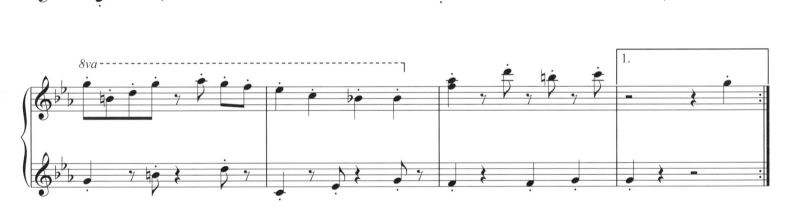

8va

1.

2.   *Count "2, 3, 4, 1"*
      with your hand

Smooth Bossa Nova (♩ = c.150-160)

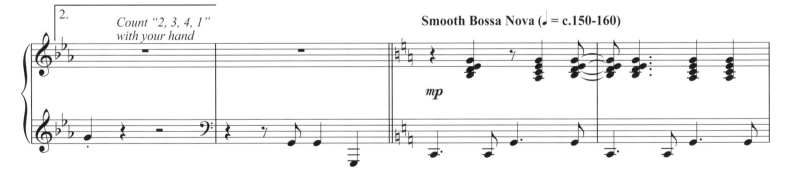

mp

FELIZ NAVIDAD
Music and Lyrics by JOSÉ FELICIANO

Optional: cut to Alternate Ending

Original Ending

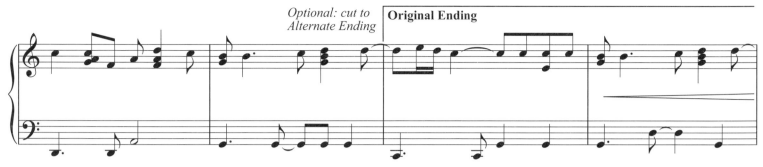

Alternate Ending
(for advanced players)

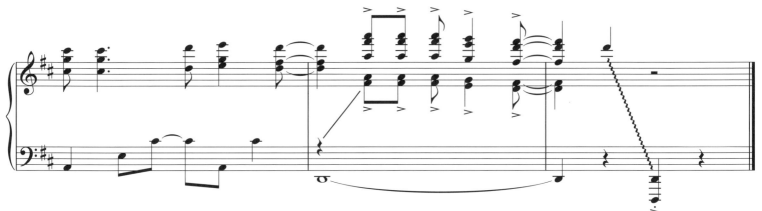

WHERE ARE YOU CHRISTMAS?/ GROWN-UP CHRISTMAS LIST

Arranged by
JASON LYLE BLACK

Thoughtfully ($\quad$ = c.92-100)

WHERE ARE YOU CHRISTMAS?
Words and Music by WILL JENNINGS, JAMES HORNER and MARIAH CAREY

Slightly faster (♩ = c.124)
GROWN-UP CHRISTMAS LIST
Words and Music by DAVID FOSTER and LINDA THOMPSON-JENNER

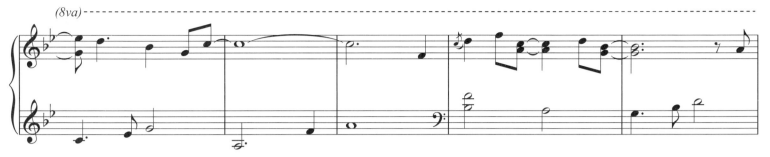

Slightly faster

60

Slowly (♩ = c.108)
WHERE ARE YOU CHRISTMAS?

JASON LYLE BLACK

is an award-winning composer, arranger, and concert pianist, whose YouTube music channel has been viewed millions of times all over the world, including features from *Yahoo*, *The Huffington Post*, *Good Morning America*, and *Buzzfeed*.

Also known as "The Backwards Piano Man"® for his musical comedy, Black has performed on "The Ellen DeGeneres Show" (Hollywood), Fuji Television (Tokyo), and in concerts throughout the United States and Canada.

As a composer, Black reached #1 and #2 on the iTunes and Billboard New Age charts. His original music, and many of his arrangements, can be heard on Spotify, Apple Music, and other streaming platforms.

Along with his touring and composing careers, Black is a frequent workshop presenter and mentor to young musicians. For more about Black's music, or to see upcoming concert dates, visit **jasonlyleblack.com**.

Photo credit: Jacq Justice